Ace Your Math Test

FRACTIONS AND DECIMALS

Ace your Math Test

Rebecca Wingard-Nelson

Enslow Publishers, Inc.
40 Industrial Road
Box 398
Berkeley Heights, NJ 07922
USA

http://www.enslow.com

Library of Congress Cataloging-in-Publication Data

Wingard-Nelson, Rebecca.
 Fractions and decimals / Rebecca Wingard-Nelson.
     p. cm. -— (Ace your math test)
 Summary: "Learn how to add, subtract, multiply, and divide both fractions and
decimals, how to convert between the two, and how to make them into percents"—
Provided by publisher.
 Includes index.
 ISBN 978-0-7660-3780-9
 1. Fractions—Juvenile literature. 2. Decimal fractions—Juvenile literature. I. Title.
 QA117.W5565 2010
 513.2'6—dc22
                                2010031015

Paperback ISBN 978-1-4644-0007-0
ePUB ISBN 978-1-4645-0454-9
PDF ISBN 978-1-4646-0454-6

Printed in the United States of America

092011 Lake Book Manufacturing, Inc., Melrose Park, IL

10 9 8 7 6 5 4 3 2 1

To Our Readers: We have done our best to make sure all Internet Addresses in this book were active and appropriate when we went to press. However, the author and the publisher have no control over and assume no liability for the material available on those Internet sites or on other Web sites they may link to. Any comments or suggestions can be sent by e-mail to comments@enslow.com or to the address on the back cover.

♻ Enslow Publishers, Inc., is committed to printing our books on recycled paper. The paper in every book contains 10% to 30% post-consumer waste (PCW). The cover board on the outside of each book contains 100% PCW. Our goal is to do our part to help young people and the environment too!

Illustration Credits: Shutterstock.com

Cover Photo: Shutterstock.com

CONTENTS

Test-Taking Tips

Be Prepared!

Most of the topics that are found on math tests are taught in the classroom. Paying attention in class, taking good notes, and keeping up with your homework are the best ways to be prepared for tests.

Practice

Use test preparation materials, such as flash cards and timed worksheets, to practice your basic math skills. Take practice tests. They show the kinds of items that will be on the actual test. They can show you what areas you understand, and what areas you need more practice in.

Test Day!

The Night Before

Relax. Eat a good meal. Go to bed early enough to get a good night's sleep. Don't cram on new material! Review the material you know is going to be on the test.

Get what you need ready. Sharpen your pencils, set out things like erasers, a calculator, and any extra materials, like books, protractors, tissues, or cough drops.

The Big Day

Get up early enough to eat breakfast and not have to hurry. Wear something that is comfortable and makes you feel good. Listen to your favorite music.

Get to school and class on time. Stay calm. Stay positive.

Test Time!

Before you begin, take a deep breath. Focus on the test, not the people or things around you. Remind yourself to do your best, and not to worry about what you do not know.

Work through the entire test, but don't spend too much time on any one problem. Don't rush, but move quickly first, answering all of the questions you can do easily. Go back a second time and answer the questions that take more time.

Read each question completely. Read all the answer choices. Eliminate answers that are obviously wrong. Read word problems carefully, and decide what the problem is asking.

Check each answer to make sure it is reasonable. Estimate numbers to see if your answer makes sense.

Concentrate on the test. Stay focused. If your attention starts to wander, take a short break. Breathe. Relax. Refocus. Don't get upset if you can't answer a question. Mark it, then come back to it later.

When you finish, look back over the entire test. Are all of the questions answered? Check as many problems as you can. Look at your calculations and make sure you have the same answer on the blank as you do on your worksheet.

Let's Go!

Three common types of test problems are covered in this book: Multiple Choice, Show Your Work, and Explain Your Answer. Tips on how to solve each, as well as common errors to avoid, are also presented. Knowing what to expect on a test and what is expected of you will have you ready to ace every math test you take.

1. Fractions

Parts and Wholes

Any part of a whole is called a fraction. A fraction can be part of one whole thing, or part of a whole group.

Definitions

denominator: The bottom number in a fraction. It tells the total number of equal parts.

numerator: The top number in a fraction. It tells the number of parts being talked about.

Eight girls spent Friday night at a slumber party. Only three of the girls went to sleep. Write a fraction to describe the number of the girls who slept.

Step 1: How many girls are in the whole group? 8. The number 8 is the bottom number, or denominator.

$$\frac{\quad}{8}$$

Step 2: How many of the girls went to sleep Friday night? 3. The number 3 is the top number, or numerator.

$$\frac{3}{8}$$

TEST TIME: Multiple Choice

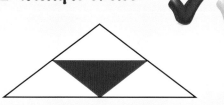

Which fraction can be used to tell how much of the large triangle is colored?

(a.) 1/4

b. 3/4

c. 4/1

d. 4/3

Extras

Fractions are written using a fraction bar or a slash.

$\frac{1}{2}$ or 1/2

When you can find the solution to a multiple choice question quickly, mark the answer and move on. This problem gives you a picture of a large triangle. It is made of four triangular sections that are the same size. The denominator of the fraction is 4. One of the four sections is colored. The numerator (top number) is 1.

Solution: The correct answer is a. Mark it, and move on.

Definitions

proper fraction: A fraction whose numerator is less than its denominator. Example: 4/9

improper fraction: A fraction whose numerator is equal to or greater than its denominator. Example: 8/5 or 5/5

Improper Fractions

Write an improper fraction to show how many large squares are shaded in color.

Step 1: The denominator of an improper fraction is the number of equal parts in one whole. How many equal parts are there in one whole square? 4. This is the denominator.

$$\frac{}{4}$$

Step 2: How many of the equal parts are shaded? 11. The number 11 is the top number, or numerator.

$$\frac{11}{4}$$

TEST TIME: Show Your Work

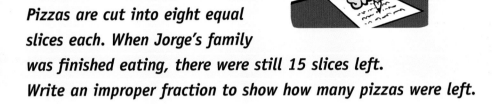

Pizzas are cut into eight equal slices each. When Jorge's family was finished eating, there were still 15 slices left. Write an improper fraction to show how many pizzas were left.

A sketch could help you understand this problem. Each pizza is cut into eight equal slices. Draw a pizza with 8 slices. You need to have 15 slices left. Draw another pizza with 8 slices. Now there are 16 slices. That is enough. Shade 15 of the slices. Now write the improper fraction. Remember, the denominator in an improper fraction is the number of equal parts in ONE whole. The denominator is 8. There are 15 slices left. The numerator is 15. Write the answer in a full sentence.

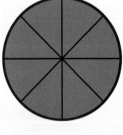

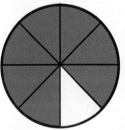

Solution: When Jorge's family was finished eating, there were 15/8 pizzas left.

Test-Taking Hint

Questions that ask you to show how you found the solution are sometimes called "Show Your Work" or "Short Answer" questions. Showing your work and showing some effort will earn you part of the credit, even if you have the wrong answer. The right answer, without showing some work, may only give you partial credit.

2. Mixed Fractions

Mixed and Improper Fractions

Mixed fractions and improper fractions are ways to show a value of one or greater.

Definition

mixed fraction: A number made of two parts: a whole number and a proper fraction. Example: $2\frac{1}{3}$

Mixed fractions and improper fractions can be used to show the same value. Look at the rectangles below.

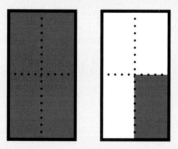

As an improper fraction, there are 4 equal parts in one whole, and 5 parts are shaded.

$$\frac{5}{4}$$

The same value can be written as a mixed fraction. The whole number part is the number of full rectangles that are shaded. There is one full rectangle. The fraction part tells the fraction for the partially shaded rectangle. There is one part of the 4 equal parts colored. The fraction part is 1/4.

$$1\frac{1}{4}$$

Renaming Improper Fractions

Any improper fraction can be renamed as a mixed fraction using division.

Write 9/2 as a mixed fraction.

Step 1: Divide the numerator by the denominator.

$$9 \div 2 = 4 \text{ remainder } 1$$

Step 2: Write the mixed fraction. The remainder is the numerator of the fraction part. The denominator stays the same as it is in the original improper fraction.

$$4\frac{1}{2}$$

Test-Taking Hint

Some multiple choice questions can be solved by eliminating choices that are obviously incorrect.

TEST TIME: Multiple Choice

Which improper fraction has the same value as 2 $\frac{1}{3}$?

      a. 2/3

      b. 3/4

      c. 5/4

      d. 7/3

This problem can be solved by eliminating answers you know are incorrect. The answer is an improper fraction. Answers a and b are both proper fractions. You can also eliminate answer c by looking at the denominator. The denominator in the improper fraction should be the same as the denominator in the fraction part of the mixed fraction.

Solution: The only possible answer is d.

Renaming Mixed Fractions

Any mixed fraction can be renamed as an improper fraction.

Write 4 $^3/_5$ as an improper fraction.

Step 1: The numerator of the improper fraction is found by multiplying the whole number by the denominator, then adding the numerator from the mixed fraction.

$$(4 \times 5) + 3 = 23$$

Step 2: Write the improper fraction. The denominator is the same as the denominator in the fraction part of the mixed fraction.

$$\frac{23}{5}$$

Test-Taking Hint

An answer in a multiple choice problem might look correct if you go too quickly. Often the wrong answers listed are ones you would find if you made a common error.

3. Equivalent Fractions

Fraction Names

Fractions can be written using different names, but they will still have the same value. Let's look at how a partially colored square can be divided into different sized equal parts.

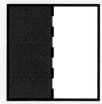

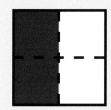

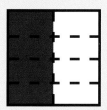

This square has 2 equal parts. One is shaded. The fraction is 1/2.

The same square now has 4 equal parts. Two are shaded. The fraction is 2/4.

The same square now has 8 equal parts. Four are shaded. The fraction is 4/8.

Definition

equivalent: Equal in value. For example, 1/2 = 2/4 = 4/8

Test-Taking Hint

Some problems ask a question, and ask you to explain your answer. Others just ask for an explanation. Your score is based on both a correct response and how clearly you explain your reasoning. If there is no direct question, try to include an example when you can.

TEST TIME: Explain Your Answer

Explain one way to find a fraction that is equivalent to 1/3.

Solution: You can multiply both the numerator and denominator by the same number without changing the value of a fraction. This is one way to find an equivalent fraction.

$$\frac{1}{3} = \frac{1 \times 2 = 2}{3 \times 2 = 6}$$

The fraction 2/6 is equivalent to 1/3.

Definitions

factors: Numbers that divide evenly into a given number. The number 2 divides evenly into 6. The number 2 is a factor of 6.

common factors: Numbers that divide evenly into a set of numbers. The number 3 divides evenly into 9 and 12. The number 3 is a common factor of 9 and 12.

greatest common factor: The largest number that divides evenly into a set of numbers.

Lowest Terms

A fraction is in lowest terms when the numerator and denominator do not have any common factors except 1.

Write 25/100 in lowest terms.

Step 1: Find the greatest common factor of the numerator, 25, and denominator, 100.

Factors of 25:   1, 5, 25
Factors of 100:   1, 2, 4, 5, 10, 20, 25, 50, 100

The common factors of 25 and 100 are 1, 5, and 25.
The greatest common factor is 25.

Step 2: Write the fraction in lowest terms by dividing the numerator and denominator by the greatest common factor, 25.

$$\frac{25}{100} = \frac{25 \div 25}{100 \div 25} = \frac{1}{4}$$

TEST TIME: Multiple Choice

Which fraction is in lowest terms?

        a. 1/4

        b. 3/8

        c. 2/9

        d. All of the above.

Check each answer to see if the numerator and denominator have any common factors other than one. Answer a: When the numerator is 1, the fraction is always in lowest terms. Answer b: The numbers 3 and 8 have no common factors except 1. Answer c: The numbers 2 and 9 have no common factors except 1.

Solution: Since answers a, b, and c are all correct, the correct choice is answer d. Answer d, all of the above, is the correct answer.

Test-Taking Hint

In multiple choice problems with the answer choice all of the above, it is best to check all of the choices.

4. Comparing Fractions

Comparing Like Fractions

Use the symbols $<$, $>$, or $=$ to compare 6/11 and 9/11.

Step 1: Only compare fractions when the denominators are equal. These two fractions have the same denominator.

$$6 < 9, \text{ so } 6/11 < 9/11$$

Definitions

like fractions: Fractions that have the same denominator.

unlike fractions: Fractions that have different denominators.

Unit Fractions

A fraction with the numerator 1 is called a unit fraction. Unit fractions can have denominators of any number. A unit is one whole. A unit fraction is part of one whole.

Think: If you cut one sandwich into two pieces, and one sandwich into eight pieces, how do the pieces compare? The 1/2 piece is larger than the 1/8 piece. 1/2 is greater than 1/8.

TEST TIME: Multiple Choice

Which of the following is a true statement?

        (a.) 1/2 > 1/3

        b. 1/2 < 1/3

        c. 1/2 = 1/3

        d. 1/3 > 1/2

1/3 and 1/2 are unit fractions. They both have a numerator of 1. The unit fraction with the larger denominator has the smaller value. 3 is larger than 2, so 1/3 is smaller than 1/2.

Solution: Answer a is correct.

Test-Taking Hint

Some problems will have the same answer in two places, just written in a different way. Answer b says 1/2 is less than 1/3. Answer d says 1/3 is greater than 1/2. These have the same meaning, but neither is correct.

Definitions

multiple: The product of a number and any whole number. Multiples of 2 are 2, 4, 6, . . .

common multiples: Numbers that are multiples of two or more numbers in a group. Some common multiples of 2 and 3 are 6, 12, and 18.

least common multiple: The smallest multiple, other than zero, that two or more numbers have in common.

Comparing Unlike Fractions

Compare $\frac{1}{3}$ and $\frac{3}{8}$.

Step 1: Write unlike fractions as like fractions using the least common denominator. Find the least common multiple of the denominators, 3 and 8.

> List the multiples of 3: 3, 6, 9, 12, 15, 18, 21, 24, . . .
> List the multiples of 8: 8, 16, 24, 32, 48, . . .
> The least common multiple of 3 and 8 is 24.

Step 2: Write both fractions with a denominator of 24. To change a denominator of 3 to a denominator of 24, multiply the numerator and denominator by 8, because 3 x 8 = 24. To change a denominator of 8 to a denominator of 24, multiply the numerator and denominator by 3, because 8 x 3 = 24.

$$\frac{1}{3} = \frac{1 \times 8}{3 \times 8} = \frac{8}{24} \qquad\qquad \frac{3}{8} = \frac{3 \times 3}{8 \times 3} = \frac{9}{24}$$

Step 3: Compare like fractions by comparing the numerators.

$$8 < 9, \text{ so } \frac{8}{24} < \frac{9}{24} \qquad\qquad \frac{1}{3} < \frac{3}{8}$$

TEST TIME: Multiple Choice

Which of the following sets is listed in order from least to greatest?

     a. 1/3, 2/3, 5/6, 1/2

     b. 1/2, 2/3, 1/3, 5/6

     c. 1/2, 1/3, 2/3, 5/6

     d. 1/3, 1/2, 2/3, 5/6

The same four fractions are listed in each answer. There are like and unlike fractions. One way to solve this problem is to write the fractions with common denominators. The least common denominator is 6.

$$1/3 = 1/3 \times 2/2 = 2/6$$
$$2/3 = 2/3 \times 2/2 = 4/6$$
$$1/2 = 1/2 \times 3/3 = 3/6$$
$$5/6 = 5/6$$

The correct order from least to greatest is
2/6, 3/6, 4/6, 5/6, or
1/3, 1/2, 2/3, 5/6
Find the answer that orders the fractions correctly. You can do this quickly by noting that the smallest fraction in the list is 1/3 and the largest fraction is 5/6. Only answer d lists 1/3 first and 5/6 last.

Solution: Check answer d against the list you made. Answer d is correct.

5. Adding Like Fractions

Proper Fractions

Add $2/7$ and $3/7$.

Step 1: To add like fractions, add only the numerators, 2 and 3.

$$2 + 3 = 5$$

Step 2: Keep the same denominator, 7.

$$5/7$$

Mixed Fractions

Add $2\ 1/4$ and $1\ 2/4$

Step 1: Add the fractions. $1/4 + 2/4 = 3/4$

Step 2: Add the whole numbers. $2 + 1 = 3$

Step 3: Add the whole number sum and the fraction sum. $3 + 3/4 = 3\ 3/4$

Test-Taking Hint

Multiple choice problems give you a list of solutions. Other kinds of problems ask you to provide the solution. Problems that ask you to provide the solution should be answered clearly and in complete sentences.

TEST TIME: Show Your Work

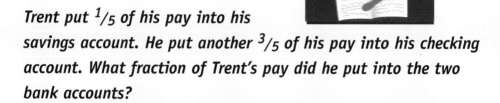

Trent put $^1/_5$ of his pay into his savings account. He put another $^3/_5$ of his pay into his checking account. What fraction of Trent's pay did he put into the two bank accounts?

A fraction of Trent's pay was put into savings and a fraction was put into checking. The problem asks for the total fraction that was put into the bank. Problems that ask for a total are often addition problems. Add the two fractions to find the answer.

$$^1/_5 + ^3/_5 = ^4/_5$$

Write the answer in a full sentence.

Solution: Trent put $^4/_5$ of his pay into the two bank accounts.

Regrouping

Add $1\frac{2}{3}$ and $2\frac{2}{3}$.

Step 1: Add the fractions.

$$\frac{2}{3} + \frac{2}{3} = \frac{4}{3}$$

Step 2: Regroup this sum. Write the improper fraction as a mixed fraction. (See page 11.)

$$\frac{4}{3} = 1\frac{1}{3}$$

Step 3: Add the whole numbers.

$$1 + 2 = 3$$

Step 4: Add the fraction sum and the whole number sum.

$$1\frac{1}{3} + 3 = 4\frac{1}{3}$$

$$1\frac{2}{3} + 2\frac{2}{3} = 4\frac{1}{3}$$

Test-Taking Hint

Write fractions in your answer in lowest terms.
Write improper fractions as whole or mixed numbers.

TEST TIME: Multiple Choice

A hiking trail is 3 $^2/_5$ miles long. A bike trail is 7 $^4/_5$ miles long. How long are the two trails combined?

a. 10 $^1/_5$ miles
b. 11 $^1/_5$ miles
c. 11 $^2/_5$ miles
d. 11 $^6/_5$ miles

To find a combined distance, add the mixed fractions. Remember to regroup the sum of the fraction parts as a mixed fraction.

3 $^2/_5$ + 7 $^4/_5$

Fraction parts:	2/5 + 4/5 = 6/5 = 1 $^1/_5$
Whole number parts:	3 + 7 = 10
Combined sum:	1 $^1/_5$ + 10 = 11 $^1/_5$

Be careful. Answers a and d could look correct. If you forget to include the regrouped whole number, answer a would look correct. Answer d included the regrouped whole, but then left the entire improper fraction in the fraction part.

Solution: Answer b is correct.

6. Adding Unlike Fractions

Unlike Proper Fractions

Unlike fractions are written as like fractions before they are added. Convert the fractions first, so that the denominators are the same.

Add 2/3 and 1/4.

Step 1: Write unlike fractions as like fractions using the least common denominator. Find the least common multiple of the denominators, 3 and 4.

> List the multiples of 3: 3, 6, 9, 12, 15, 18, . . .
> List the multiples of 4: 4, 8, 12, 16, 20, . . .
> The least common multiple of 3 and 4 is 12.

Write both fractions with a denominator of 12.

$$\frac{2}{3} = \frac{2 \times 4}{3 \times 4} = \frac{8}{12} \qquad \frac{1}{4} = \frac{1 \times 3}{4 \times 3} = \frac{3}{12}$$

Step 2: Write the problem using the equivalent like fractions.

$$\frac{2}{3} + \frac{1}{4} \quad \text{is the same as} \quad \frac{8}{12} + \frac{3}{12}$$

Step 3: Add.

$$\frac{8}{12} + \frac{3}{12} = \frac{8 + 3}{12} = \frac{11}{12}$$

TEST TIME: Explain Your Answer

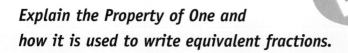

*Explain the Property of One and
how it is used to write equivalent fractions.*

Solution: The Property of One says that when you multiply any
number by 1, the value of the number does not change. For example,
$2 \times 1 = 2$ or $257 \times 1 = 257$.

A fraction with the same numerator and denominator has a value
of 1. For example, $2/2 = 1$, or $19/19 = 1$. When you write an
equivalent fraction, you multiply the numerator and denominator by
the same number. This is the same as multiplying the fraction by 1.
The value of the fraction does not change.

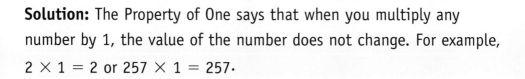

$$\frac{2}{5} = \frac{2 \times 2}{5 \times 2} = \frac{4}{10} \quad \text{So,} \frac{2}{5} = \frac{4}{10}$$

2/2 = 1

TEST TIME: Multiple Choice

Harold starting painting the rooms inside his home. On Monday, he painted 2 $\frac{1}{5}$ rooms. On Tuesday, he painted another 1 $\frac{1}{4}$ rooms. How many rooms had Harold painted by Tuesday night?

a. 2 $\frac{9}{20}$

b. 3 $\frac{1}{5}$

c. 3 $\frac{1}{9}$

d. 3 $\frac{9}{20}$

You can eliminate answer a immediately by understanding that the whole number of rooms alone is greater than 2 $\frac{9}{20}$. Answers b and c may also be quickly eliminated by knowing addition of the fraction part is $\frac{1}{5} + \frac{1}{4}$. Answer b adds the whole numbers, but only includes one of the fraction parts. Answer c adds the whole numbers, but the fraction part is less than either of the fraction parts in the two addends. The only answer left is answer d.

Solution: Answer d is correct.

You can check the answer to this problem by doing the addition. Write 2 $\frac{1}{5}$ and 1 $\frac{1}{4}$ using the least common denominator, 20, then add.

$$2 \frac{1}{5} + 1 \frac{1}{4} = 2 \frac{4}{20} + 1 \frac{5}{20} = 3 \frac{9}{20}$$

More Than Two Addends

When more than two fractions are added, the denominator must be common to all of the fractions.

Add $\frac{1}{5}$ and $\frac{1}{10}$ and $\frac{1}{2}$.

Step 1: Write unlike fractions as like fractions using the least common denominator. Find the least common multiple of the denominators, 2, 5, and 10.

List the multiples of 2: 2, 4, 6, 8, 10, 12, . . .
List the multiples of 5: 5, 10, 15, 20, 25, . . .
List the multiples of 10: 10, 20, 30, 40, 50, . . .
The least common multiple of the three denominators is 10.

Write each fraction with a denominator of 10.

$$\frac{1}{5} = \frac{1 \times 2}{5 \times 2} = \frac{2}{10} \qquad \frac{1}{10} = \frac{1}{10} \qquad \frac{1}{2} = \frac{1 \times 5}{2 \times 5} = \frac{5}{10}$$

Step 2: Write the problem using the equivalent like fractions.

$$\frac{1}{5} + \frac{1}{10} + \frac{1}{2} \quad \text{is the same as} \quad \frac{2}{10} + \frac{1}{10} + \frac{5}{10}$$

Step 3: Add.

$$\frac{2}{10} + \frac{1}{10} + \frac{5}{10} = \frac{2 + 1 + 5}{10} = \frac{8}{10}$$

Step 4: Reduce to lowest terms.

$$\frac{8}{10} = \frac{4}{5}$$

7. Subtracting Like Fractions

Subtracting Proper Fractions

Fractions are subtracted the same way they are added.

Find the difference between 7/12 and 5/12.

Step 1: To subtract like fractions, subtract only the numerators.

$$7 - 5 = 2$$

Step 2: Keep the same denominator, 12.

$$2/12$$

Step 3: Reduce to lowest terms.

$$\frac{2}{12} = \frac{1}{6}$$

Test-Taking Hint

Word problems, or story problems, should be answered in complete sentences.

TEST TIME: Show Your Work

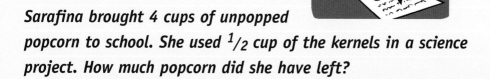

Sarafina brought 4 cups of unpopped popcorn to school. She used $^1/_2$ cup of the kernels in a science project. How much popcorn did she have left?

Regroup 4 cups so that one of the cups is written as an improper fraction with a denominator of 2.

$4 = 3\ ^2/_2$

Rewrite the problem.

Subtract the fraction part.

Bring down the whole number.

$$
\begin{array}{r}
3\ ^2/_2 \\
-\ ^1/_2 \\
\hline
3\ ^1/_2
\end{array}
$$

Write the answer in a full sentence.

Solution: Sarafina has $3\ ^1/_2$ cups of popcorn left.

TEST TIME: Multiple Choice

Subtract 5 – ³/8.

     a. 3 ⁵/8
     b. 4 ⁵/8
     c. 5 ³/9
     d. 5 ⁵/8

When you subtract, the result is less than the original number. You can eliminate answers c and d by understanding that they are greater than the original number. Answer a can also be eliminated. The fraction that is being subtracted is less than one. If less than one is taken from 5, the result will be greater than 4.

Another way to solve this problem is to use the inverse operation of addition. Look at the remaining answers, a and b. Which of these when added to the fraction ³/8 will result in the original number, 5? Answer a will result in 4, answer b will result in 5.

Solution: Answer b is correct.

Test-Taking Hint

Mixed fractions, as well as fractions, should always be reduced to lowest terms. Both forms are correct, but an answer in lowest terms is better.

Subtracting Mixed Fractions

Mixed fractions may need to be regrouped before they can be subtracted.

Breanna took 6 $^5/_6$ hours to read a book. Keith took 8 $^1/_6$ hours to read the same book. How much longer did Keith take to read the book?

Step 1: Use subtraction to find the difference in the number of hours. The numerator 5 is greater than the numerator 1. Regroup the whole number 8 as 7 $^6/_6$.

$$8 \, ^1/_6 = 7 + \, ^6/_6 + \, ^1/_6 = \quad 7 \, ^7/_6$$
$$-\, 6 \, ^5/_6 \qquad\qquad\qquad\qquad -\, 6 \, ^5/_6$$

Step 2: Subtract.

$$7 \, ^7/_6$$
$$-\, 6 \, ^5/_6$$
$$\overline{1 \, ^2/_6}$$

Step 3: Reduce to lowest terms.

$$1 \, ^2/_6 = 1 \, ^1/_3$$

Keith took 1 $^1/_3$ hours longer to read the book than Breanna did.

8. Subtracting Unlike Fractions

Unlike Proper Fractions

Unlike fractions are subtracted in the same way as they are added. Change the fractions first, so that the denominators are the same.

Subtract 3/4 − 1/2.

Step 1: Write unlike fractions as like fractions using the least common denominator. Find the least common multiple of the denominators, 2 and 4.

List the multiples of 2: 2, 4, 6, 8, 10, 12, . . .
List the multiples of 4: 4, 8, 12, 16, . . .

Write each fraction with a denominator of 4.

$$\frac{1}{2} = \frac{1 \times 2}{2 \times 2} = \frac{2}{4} \qquad\qquad \frac{3}{4} = \frac{3}{4}$$

Step 2: Write the problem using the equivalent like fractions.

$$\frac{3}{4} - \frac{2}{4}$$

Step 3: Subtract.

$$\frac{3}{4} - \frac{2}{4} = \frac{1}{4}$$

TEST TIME: Multiple Choice

Which of the following is NOT correct?

      a. $11/12 - 1/3 = 7/12$

      b. $2/3 - 1/2 = 1/6$

      (c.) $13/15 - 2/5 = 4/15$

      d. $5/7 - 3/10 = 29/70$

This problem asks you to find the equation that is not correct. Three of the four ARE correct. None of these answers is easy to eliminate.

One way to solve this problem is to solve each equation. Remember, you are looking for the equation that is NOT correct.

a. $11/12 - 1/3 = 11/12 - 4/12 = 7/12$

b. $2/3 - 1/2 = 4/6 - 3/6 = 1/6$

c. $13/15 - 2/5 = 13/15 - 6/15 = 7/15$

d. $5/7 - 3/10 = 50/70 - 21/70 = 29/70$

Solution: The only equation that is not correct is in answer c.

Mixed Fractions

Subtract 3 2/3 and 1 1/6.

Step 1: Write the problem using like fractions.

$$3\ 2/3 \qquad 3\ 4/6$$
$$-\ 1\ 1/6 \qquad -\ 1\ 1/6$$

Step 2: Subtract the fractions.

$$3\ 4/6$$
$$-\ 1\ 1/6$$
$$\overline{\qquad 3/6}$$

Step 3: Subtract the whole numbers.

$$3\ 4/6$$
$$-\ 1\ 1/6$$
$$\overline{\quad 2\ 3/6}$$

Step 4: Reduce the fraction to lowest terms. $2\ 3/6\ =\ 2\ 1/2$

Test-Taking Hint

In a hurry? Find a common denominator by multiplying the denominators of the two fractions. In 2/6 and 1/8, the denominators are 6 and 8. A common denominator is 6 x 8 = 48. Since this is not always the least common denominator, be sure to reduce your answer to lowest terms.

TEST TIME: Show Your Work

The perimeter of a triangle is 16 1/3 feet. The lengths of two of the sides are 6 1/2 feet and 2 1/3 feet. How long is the third side?

The perimeter of a triangle is the total distance around the triangle. One way to find the length of the third side is to add the two sides that are given, and subtract the sum from the perimeter. Another way is to subtract one of the side lengths from the perimeter, then subtract the second. In this case, since one of the sides has the same fraction part as the perimeter, it is easier to subtract that side length first.

Perimeter $-$ side length (1) $-$ side length (2) = side length (3)

$16 \frac{1}{3}$ ft $-$ $2 \frac{1}{3}$ ft $-$ $6 \frac{1}{2}$ ft = side length (3)

14 ft $-$ $6 \frac{1}{2}$ ft = side length (3)

$13 \frac{2}{2}$ ft $-$ $6 \frac{1}{2}$ ft = side length (3)

$7 \frac{1}{2}$ ft = side length (3)

Solution: The length of the third side is $7 \frac{1}{2}$ feet.

9. Multiplying Fractions

Like or Unlike Fractions

Multiplication of like and unlike fractions is done in the same way.

Like Fractions

Multiply 1/4 × 3/4.

Step 1: Multiply the numerators.

$$\frac{1}{4} \times \frac{3}{4} = \frac{1 \times 3}{} = \frac{3}{}$$

Step 2: Multiply the denominators.

$$\frac{1}{4} \times \frac{3}{4} = \frac{1 \times 3}{4 \times 4} = \frac{3}{16}$$

Unlike Fractions

Multiply 1/3 × 5/8.

Step 1: Multiply the numerators.

$$\frac{1}{3} \times \frac{5}{8} = \frac{1 \times 5}{} = \frac{5}{}$$

Step 2: Multiply the denominators.

$$\frac{1}{3} \times \frac{5}{8} = \frac{1 \times 5}{3 \times 8} = \frac{5}{24}$$

TEST TIME: Show Your Work

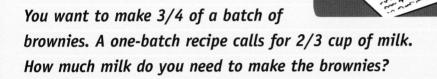

You want to make 3/4 of a batch of brownies. A one-batch recipe calls for 2/3 cup of milk. How much milk do you need to make the brownies?

To make 3/4 of a batch, you need to use 3/4 of each ingredient. It may help you to write this in words. To make 3/4 of a batch of brownies, you need 3/4 of 2/3 cup of milk for one batch. The word "of" in this problem means multiplication.

$$3/4 \text{ of } 2/3 \text{ cup} = 3/4 \times 2/3$$

Multiply the numerators.
Multiply the denominators.

$$\frac{3 \times 2}{4 \times 3} = \frac{6}{12}$$

Reduce to lowest terms.

$$\frac{6}{12} = \frac{1}{2}$$

Solution: You need 1/2 cup of milk to make the brownies.

Whole Numbers and Fractions

Multiply 16 and 3/4.

Step 1: Write the whole number as an improper fraction with a denominator of 1.

$$\frac{16}{1} \times \frac{3}{4}$$

Step 2: Simplify by dividing the numerator of one fraction and the denominator of the other by a common factor. In this problem, you can divide 16 by 4, and 4 by 4.

$$\overset{4}{\cancel{\frac{16}{1}}} \times \frac{3}{\underset{1}{\cancel{4}}}$$

Step 3: Multiply the numerators and multiply the denominators.

$$\frac{4}{1} \times \frac{3}{1} = \frac{4 \times 3}{1 \times 1} = \frac{12}{1} = 12$$

TEST TIME: Multiple Choice

Ian's car averages 25 miles per gallon of fuel. He has exactly 5 $\frac{1}{5}$ gallons of fuel in his tank. How far can Ian drive before he runs out of fuel?

> a. 125 miles
> b. 130 miles
> c. 130 $\frac{1}{5}$ miles
> d. 135 miles

To find the distance Ian can drive, multiply the number of gallons of fuel in his tank by the number of miles he can drive per gallon. One way to solve this problem is to convert the whole number and the mixed fraction into improper fractions.

$$25 \times 5\frac{1}{5} = \frac{\overset{5}{\cancel{25}}}{1} \times \frac{26}{\underset{1}{\cancel{5}}} = 130$$

Solution: Answer b is correct.

Test-Taking Hint

When a question is taking an especially long time, or has you stumped, leave it and go on. Come back later if you have time.

10. Dividing Fractions

Definition

reciprocals: Two numbers that have a product of 1.
For example, 1/3 and 3/1 are reciprocals because $1/3 \times 3/1 = 1$.

Dividing a Fraction by a Fraction

Divide 1/4 by 2/5.

Step 1: Write the problem using the division sign.

$$\frac{1}{4} \div \frac{2}{5}$$

Step 2: Rewrite the problem using a multiplication sign and the reciprocal of the divisor.

$$\frac{1}{4} \times \frac{5}{2}$$

Step 3: Multiply.

$$\frac{1}{4} \times \frac{5}{2} = \frac{1 \times 5}{4 \times 2} = \frac{5}{8}$$

Dividing a Whole Number by a Fraction

To divide a whole number by a fraction, write the whole number as a fraction first.

Nan had 12 feet of fabric cut into pieces 2/3 of a foot long. How many pieces of fabric did Nan have after it was cut?

Step 1: The total fabric was divided into 2/3-foot pieces. Write this as a division problem.

12 feet ÷ 2/3-foot pieces = number of pieces
12 ÷ 2/3

Step 2: Write the whole number as an improper fraction.

$$\frac{12}{1} \div \frac{2}{3}$$

Step 3: Rewrite the problem using a multiplication sign and the reciprocal of the divisor.

$$\frac{\overset{6}{\cancel{12}}}{1} \times \frac{3}{\underset{1}{\cancel{2}}}$$

Step 4: Multiply.

$$\frac{6}{1} \times \frac{3}{1} = \frac{6 \times 3}{1 \times 1} = \frac{18}{1}$$

Nan had 18 pieces of fabric.

TEST TIME: Explain Your Answer

A flea market is being held on the high school track. The track is 1/4 mile long. If 20 booths are set up, how much space does each booth receive in miles? How much space does each booth receive in feet? Explain how you found your answer.

This problem asks for two measurement answers: one in miles, and one in feet. It also asks for an explanation of how you found the answers. Be sure to include all of the required parts.

Solution: The track is 1/4 mile long, divided into 20 sections for booths. To find the amount of space each booth gets in miles, you must divide 1/4 mile by 20.

$$1/4 \div 20 = 1/4 \times 1/20 = 1/80$$

Each booth has 1/80 of a mile of space.

There are 5,280 feet in a mile.
To find the amount of space each booth gets in feet, you can multiply the number of feet in a mile by the fraction of a mile for each booth.

$$5,280 \times 1/80 = 5,280/1 \times 1/80 = 66 \text{ feet}$$

Each booth has 66 feet of space.

Fractions that have 1 in the numerator can be divided easily. Just multiply the dividend by the denominator. For example, dividing by 1/2 is the same as multiplying by 2.

Mixed Fractions

Divide 4 $\frac{1}{2}$ by 1 $\frac{1}{4}$.

Step 1: Write each mixed fraction as an improper fraction.

$$4\frac{1}{2} \div 1\frac{1}{4} = \frac{9}{2} \div \frac{5}{4}$$

Step 2: Rewrite the problem using a multiplication sign and the reciprocal of the divisor.

$$\frac{9}{\underset{1}{\cancel{2}}} \times \frac{\overset{2}{\cancel{4}}}{5}$$

Step 3: Multiply.

$$\frac{9}{1} \times \frac{2}{5} = \frac{9 \times 2}{1 \times 5} = \frac{18}{5}$$

Step : Write the improper fraction as a mixed number.

$$\frac{18}{5} = 3\frac{3}{5}$$

11. Estimating With Fractions

Estimate Fractions

One way to estimate the answer to a problem that uses fractions is to use fractions that work well together. For example, like fractions are easy to add and subtract.

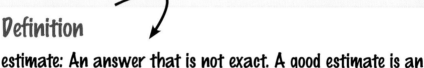

Definition

estimate: An answer that is not exact. A good estimate is an answer that is close to the exact answer.

Estimate Addition

Estimate the sum of 1/12, 1/14, and 1/13.

Step 1: 1/12 and 1/14 are both close to 1/13. 1/13 is one of the addends. Change 1/12 to 1/13 and 1/14 to 1/13.

$$\frac{1}{12} + \frac{1}{13} + \frac{1}{14} \text{ is close to } \frac{1}{13} + \frac{1}{13} + \frac{1}{13}$$

Step 2: Use mental math.

$$\frac{1}{13} + \frac{1}{13} + \frac{1}{13} = \frac{3}{13}$$

$$\frac{1}{12} + \frac{1}{13} + \frac{1}{14} \text{ is about } \frac{3}{13}$$

TEST TIME: Multiple Choice

Which of the following is NOT a good reason to estimate?
- a. Because you don't need an exact answer.
- (b.) Because you don't want to solve the problem.
- c. To predict what the answer might be.
- d. To check if an answer is reasonable.

This problem asks you to decide which reason is NOT a good one to find an estimate.

When you don't need an exact answer, you want to predict the answer, or you want to check if your answer is reasonable are all good reasons to estimate. Not wanting to solve a problem is NOT a good reason to estimate.

Solution: The correct answer is b.

Test-Taking Hint

Not all of the questions on a math test need computations. Know math definitions and know the reasons behind the math.

TEST TIME: Explain Your Answer

Jenna is making headbands for her team of 4 people in an obstacle course. Each headband uses 3/16 of a yard of fabric. Should Jenna overestimate or underestimate to find the amount of fabric to buy? Why? About how much fabric should she buy?

This problem asks three questions. Be sure to answer each in your solution. An overestimate is a little larger than the exact solution. An underestimate is a little smaller than the exact solution.

Solution: When you need to be sure you have enough of something, like money, or in this case fabric, you should overestimate. To overestimate, make the fraction 3/16 a little larger, to 4/16 or 1/4.

Jenna needs 4 headbands, each using about 1/4 of a yard of fabric. 4/1 and 1/4 are reciprocals, so their product is 1.

Jenna should purchase about 1 yard of fabric.

Round to Whole Numbers

One way to estimate the answer to a problem that uses mixed fractions is to round each mixed fraction to the nearest whole number.

Estimate the product of 14 $\frac{1}{3}$ and 29 $\frac{3}{4}$.

Step 1: Find the nearest whole number to each mixed fraction.

$14\frac{1}{3}$ rounds to **14.** $29\frac{3}{4}$ rounds to **30.**

Step 2: Multiply the whole numbers.

$$14 \times 30 = 420$$

The product of $14\frac{1}{3}$ and $29\frac{1}{4}$ is about 420.

The exact answer to this problem is $426\frac{5}{12}$. 420 is a good estimate.

12. Decimals

Definition

decimal: A number based on ten. In a decimal, a decimal point separates whole number values from values less than one.

16.23
whole number.less than one

Place Value

Decimals and whole numbers have the same place value pattern. Each place has a value that is ten times the place on its right.

What is the value of digit 3 in this decimal?
85.631

Step 1: Find the digit 3 in the decimal.

85.6<u>3</u>1

Step 2: Determine what place the digit is in. The 3 is two places to the right of the decimal point. This is the hundredths place.

The digit 3 in the decimal 85.631 has a value of 3 hundredths.

TEST TIME: Multiple Choice

Which is the correct word form of the decimal 5.047?

   a. five and forty-seven thousandths
   b. five and forty-seven hundredths
   c. five thousand forty-seven
   d. five and forty-seven thousands

Decimals are read and written in words by saying the whole number value first, reading the decimal point as "and," reading the number after the decimal point as a whole number, then finally saying the place value name of the last digit.

The whole number is five and the number after the decimal point is forty-seven. The final digit, 7, is in the thousandths place.

Solution: The correct answer is a.

Test-Taking Hint

All of the decimal place names after the decimal point end in "ths." Tenths, hundredths, thousandths, ten-thousandths . . .

Equivalent Decimals

Write an equivalent decimal for each of the following numbers: 0.4, 3, and 1.6.

Step 1: Equivalent decimals are written by adding zeros to the right of the decimal point. Add one zero to the right of 0.4.

$$0.4 = 0.40$$

Step 2: Whole numbers have a decimal point to the right of the whole number. Write in the decimal point, then add a zero after the decimal point.

$$3 = 3.0$$

Step 3: You can add any number of zeros to form equivalent decimals. Add two zeros to the right of 1.6.

$$1.6 = 1.600$$

TEST TIME: Show Your Work

Name the decimal for each illustration.

  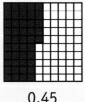

Solution: 0.4   0.40   0.45

Decimals are like fractions. They represent part of a whole. In a decimal, the parts are always related to ten: tenths, hundredths, thousandths, and so on.

The first illustration shows four out of ten parts shaded. This is read as four tenths, and written as 0.4.

The second illustration shows forty out of one hundred parts shaded. This is read as forty hundredths, and written as 0.40.

The third illustration shows forty-five out of one hundred parts shaded. This is read as forty-five hundredths and written as 0.45.

13. Decimals as Fractions

Decimals to Fractions

Decimals and fractions sound the same when they are read out loud. When you hear someone say "two hundredths," are they reading the fraction 2/100 or the decimal 0.02?

Write 0.72 as a fraction.

Step 1: The digits to the right of the decimal point are the numerator. Write 72 as the numerator.

$$72$$

Step 2: The place value of the last digit tells you the denominator. The last digit is 2. The 2 is in the hundredths place, so write 100 in the denominator.

$$\frac{72}{100}$$

Step 3: Reduce the fraction to lowest terms. Divide 72 and 100 by 4.

$$\frac{72 \div 4}{100 \div 4} = \frac{18}{25}$$

Which fraction in lowest terms is equivalent to 0.175?

   a. 1/8
   b. 7/40
   c. 35/200
   d. 175/1,000

The decimal 0.175 is the same as the fraction 175/1,000. This can be reduced to lowest terms by dividing each term by 25.

Solution: The correct answer is b.

Test-Taking Hint

Pay more attention to the question you are working on than to the amount of time left for the test.

Put a small mark next to answers you're not sure of. When you finish your test, go back and check those problems first.

Reducing More Than Once

Sometimes it's hard to find the greatest common factor. You can reduce a fraction as many times as you need. Use any common factor first. Keep reducing until the fraction is in lowest terms.

Write 0.68 as a fraction.

Step 1: The numerator is 68 and the denominator is 100.

$$\frac{68}{100}$$

Step 2: Reduce the fraction. An easy common factor for even numbers is 2. Divide 68 and 100 by 2 first.

$$\frac{68 \div 2}{100 \div 2} = \frac{34}{50}$$

Step 3: Reduce the fraction again. Both of the new numbers are even. Divide by the common factor 2 again. The fraction is now in lowest terms.

$$\frac{34 \div 2}{50 \div 2} = \frac{17}{25}$$

TEST TIME: Explain Your Answer

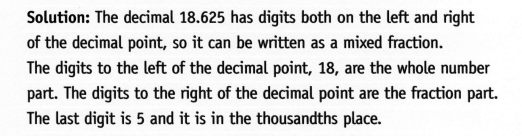

It took Tina 18.625 gallons of fuel to fill her tank. How many gallons is this as a fraction? Explain your work.

Solution: The decimal 18.625 has digits both on the left and right of the decimal point, so it can be written as a mixed fraction. The digits to the left of the decimal point, 18, are the whole number part. The digits to the right of the decimal point are the fraction part. The last digit is 5 and it is in the thousandths place.

$$18 \tfrac{625}{1000}$$

The fraction $\tfrac{625}{1000}$ is reduced to $\tfrac{5}{8}$.

$$18 \tfrac{5}{8}$$

It took Tina $18\tfrac{5}{8}$ gallons of fuel to fill her tank.

14. Fractions as Decimals

Power of Ten Denominators

When a fraction has a power of ten in the denominator, it can easily be written as a decimal.

Write 93/100 as a decimal.

Step 1: There is no whole number part in the fraction. Write a zero to the left of the decimal point as a place holder.

0.

Step 2: The denominator is 100, so the decimal will end in the hundredths place. Write the number so that the final digit, 3, is in the hundredths place.

0.93

Which decimal has the same value as 9/1,000?

 a. 9,000

 b. 0.9

 c. 0.09

 d. 0.009

The denominator in the fraction is 1,000. Written as a decimal, the digits should end in the thousandths place.

Solution: The correct answer is d.

Test-Taking Hint

Work at your own pace. Don't worry about how fast anyone else is taking the same test.

Division

The fraction bar, or fraction slash, is one way to show division. You can use division to write any fraction as a decimal. Divide the numerator by the denominator.

Write 3/16 as a decimal.

Step 1: 3/16 means 3 ÷ 16. Write this using the long division symbol.

$$16\overline{)3}$$

Step 2: Write the dividend (the number you are dividing) as a decimal. Remember, you can add zeros to the right of a decimal number without changing the value of the number.

$$16\overline{)3.0}$$

Step 3: Divide the same way you divide whole numbers. Add zeros on the right until there is no remainder.

3/16 = 0.1875

```
        0.1875
   16 )3.0000
      - 16
        140
      - 128
        120
       - 112
          80
        - 80
           0
```

TEST TIME: Show Your Work

Write $3\frac{1}{4}$ as a decimal.

The whole number part of the mixed fraction is the whole number part of the decimal. Look at the fraction part. The denominator is 4. You can write an equivalent fraction with a denominator that is a power of ten by multiplying both the numerator and denominator by 25.

Solution: $\dfrac{1}{4} = \dfrac{1 \times 25}{4 \times 25} = \dfrac{25}{100}$

$3\dfrac{1}{4} = 3.25$

Test-Taking Hint

A calculator is a useful tool when converting fractions to decimals. It can be used to find the decimal, or it can be used to check your calculations.

15. Comparing Decimals

Using Place Value

Decimals are compared using place value in the same way that whole numbers are.

Use the symbols <, >, or = to compare 0.54 and 0.525.

Step 1: To compare decimals, you must compare the digits from left to right. It may help you to write the decimals so that the decimal points line up.

0.54
0.525

Step 2: The decimals being compared have a different number of digits. If it helps, you can add zeros on the right to make the numbers have the same number of digits.

0.540
0.525

Step 3: Compare the digits from left to right. The ones place and tenths place digits are the same in both numbers. In the hundredths place, the 4 is greater than the 2, so 0.54 is greater than 0.525.

0.54 > 0.525

TEST TIME: Show Your Work

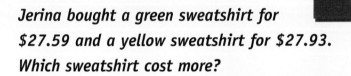

Jerina bought a green sweatshirt for $27.59 and a yellow sweatshirt for $27.93. Which sweatshirt cost more?

To solve this problem, you must compare the two dollar amounts. Dollar values that are written as decimals always have two numbers to the right of the decimal point. If it helps, line up the decimal points and compare the digits from left to right. The digits in the tens and ones place are the same. In the tenths place, 9 is greater than 5, so $27.93 is greater than $27.59.

Remember to write the answer using a complete sentence.

Solution: $27.93 > $27.59

The yellow sweatshirt cost more than the green sweatshirt.

TEST TIME: Multiple Choice

Order the decimals 0.615, 1.2, 0.127, and 0.67 from least to greatest.

> a. 1.2, 0.67, 0.127, 0.615
> b. 0.67, 0.127, 0.615, 1.2
> c. 0.127, 0.615, 0.67, 1.2
> d. 0.127, 0.67, 0.615, 1.2

You can line up the decimal points	0.615
to compare. Add zeros as necessary.	1.200
Only one number has any digits in	0.127
the ones place. 1.2 is the greatest	0.670

number, and is the last in the ordered list.
Compare the remaining numbers.
In the tenths place, 1 is less than 6. So 0.127 is the least, or smallest number. It is first in the ordered list.
The remaining two numbers both have a 6 in the tenths place. In the hundredths place, 1 is less than 7, so the next smallest number is 0.615. It is second on the list.
That leaves only 0.67 as the third number on the list.

Solution: The correct answer is c.

Find a Number

Find a number between 0.26 and 0.27.

Step 1: To find a number between two decimal numbers, you can add a zero to the right side of each to make equivalent decimals.

$$0.260$$
$$0.270$$

Step 2: Now it is easy to see that by adding a digit other than zero to the right of 0.26, you have a number greater than 0.26, and less than 0.27. Let's add a 7.

$$0.267$$

16. Adding Decimals

Place Value Columns

Decimals are added by adding only digits with the same place value.

Add 0.13 and 0.62.

Step 1: Write the numbers in a column. Line up the decimal points. When the decimal points are lined up, the place values are also lined up.

$$
\begin{array}{r}
0.13 \\
+\ 0.62 \\
\hline
\end{array}
$$

Step 2: Add the hundredths. Add the tenths.

$$
\begin{array}{r}
0.13 \\
+\ 0.62 \\
\hline
75 \\
\end{array}
$$

Step 3: Write the decimal point in the answer. Add the ones.

$$
\begin{array}{r}
0.13 \\
+\ 0.62 \\
\hline
0.75 \\
\end{array}
$$

TEST TIME: Multiple Choice

1.62 + 6.104 = _____

        a. 6.266

        b. 6.724

        c. 7.706

        d. 7.724

Write the numbers in a column. These numbers have a different number of digits on the right of the decimal point. Be very careful to add only digits that have the same place value. Line up the decimal points. You may use zeros as place holders to write the addends.

$$
\begin{array}{r}
1.620 \\
+\ 6.104 \\
\hline
7.724
\end{array}
$$

Solution: The correct answer is d.

TEST TIME: Show Your Work

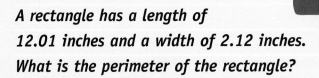

A rectangle has a length of 12.01 inches and a width of 2.12 inches. What is the perimeter of the rectangle?

Perimeter is the distance around a shape. A rectangle has four sides, two of each length. Add the four lengths to find the perimeter.

Remember to show your work and to write the answer in a complete sentence.

Solution: 12.01 + 12.01 + 2.12 + 2.12

```
  12.01
  12.01          The perimeter of the rectangle is 28.26 inches.
   2.12
+  2.12
-------
  28.26
```

Test-Taking Hint

Read problems carefully. Decide how you can use
the information given to solve the problem.

Adding Money

Add $16.52 and $31.27.

Step 1: Money amounts are added like other decimals.
Write the decimals in a column.

$$\begin{array}{r} \$16.52 \\ + \$31.27 \\ \hline \end{array}$$

Step 2: Add the digits in each place, beginning on the right.

$$\begin{array}{r} \$16.52 \\ + \$31.27 \\ \hline \$47.79 \end{array}$$

17. Regrouping to Add

Definition

regrouping: Using place value to rename values. For example: 10 ones can be regrouped as 1 ten, and 10 tenths can be regrouped as 1 one.

Regrouping in Addition

Add 0.24 and 0.68.

Step 1: Write the numbers in a column. Line up the decimal points. When the decimal points are lined up, the place values are also lined up.

$$\begin{array}{r} 0.24 \\ +\ 0.68 \\ \hline \end{array}$$

Step 2: Add the hundredths. 8 + 4 = 12. Regroup 12 hundredths as 1 tenth and 2 hundredths.

$$\begin{array}{r} 1 \\ 0.24 \\ +\ 0.68 \\ \hline 2 \end{array}$$

Step 3: Add the tenths. Include the regrouped 1 from the hundredths. Bring down the decimal point and add the ones.

$$\begin{array}{r} 1 \\ 0.24 \\ + \ 0.68 \\ \hline 0.92 \end{array}$$

TEST TIME: Multiple Choice

6.34 + 12.84 = _____

      a. 76.24

      b. 19.18

      c. 7.624

      d. 1.918

Write the numbers in a column. Line up the decimal points.

$$\begin{array}{r} 6.34 \\ + \ 12.84 \\ \hline 19.18 \end{array}$$

Solution: The correct answer is b.

TEST TIME: Show Your Work

A catering service charges per person by the items you choose from the menu. Kristina and Travis selected the baked chicken, garlic potatoes, and green salad. What is the cost per person?

Item	Cost
Baked chicken	$3.50
Glazed ham	$3.25
Garlic potatoes	$2.25
Rice pilaf	$1.75
Green beans	$1.25
Green salad	$1.75
Caesar salad	$2.25

Some of the information you need to solve a problem may be given in a table, graph, chart, or picture. This problem requires you to find the cost of the menu items on the table before you can add.

Solution:

Baked chicken:	$3.50
Garlic potatoes:	$2.25
Green salad:	+ $1.75
	$7.50

The cost per person is $7.50.

Grouping

Addition problems with more than two addends can be done by grouping some of the addends and adding them first.

Add $22.25, $20.75, and $36.15.

Step 1: You can group the first two decimal numbers in this addition problem easily in your head. Think of the decimal part of each money value as quarters. In $22.25, there are 22 dollars and one quarter. In $20.75, there are 20 dollars and 75 cents, or three quarters. Combine those values in your head. One quarter and three quarters is one dollar. There are 22 dollars and 20 dollars, and one more for the combined quarters. 22 + 20 = 1 = $43.00

Step 2: Add the sum of the first two values from step one, $43.00, and the third value, $36.15.

$$
\begin{array}{r}
\$43.00 \\
+\ \$36.15 \\
\hline
\$79.15
\end{array}
$$

18. Subtracting Decimals

Definitions

decimal numbers: Numbers that include a decimal point. Usually these are just called decimals.

decimal fractions: Decimals that have a value less than one. Decimal fractions have a zero in the ones place.

mixed decimals: Decimals that have a value greater than one. Mixed decimals have digits other than zero on both sides of the decimal point.

Subtracting by Place Value

Subtract 0.98 − 0.63.

Step 1: Subtract decimals in the same way as whole numbers. Write the decimals in a column to line up the decimal points.

$$
\begin{array}{r}
0.98 \\
-\ 0.63 \\
\hline
\end{array}
$$

Step 2: Subtract one place value at a time. Begin on the right. Subtract the hundredths.

$$
\begin{array}{r}
0.98 \\
-\ 0.63 \\
\hline
5 \\
\end{array}
$$

Step 3: Subtract the tenths.

$$
\begin{array}{r}
0.98 \\
-\ 0.63 \\
\hline
35
\end{array}
$$

Step 4: Write the decimal point in the answer. Subtract the ones.

$$
\begin{array}{r}
0.98 \\
-\ 0.63 \\
\hline
0.35
\end{array}
$$

TEST TIME: Show Your Work

Subtract 2.72 − 0.3.

This problem has decimal numbers with different numbers of digits. Be careful to line up the decimal points in decimal addition and subtraction. Remember, you can always add zeros to the right of a decimal number without changing the value.

Solution:

$$
\begin{array}{r}
2.72 \\
-\ 0.3 \\
\hline
\end{array}
\qquad
\begin{array}{r}
2.72 \\
-\ 0.30 \\
\hline
2.42
\end{array}
$$

2.72 − 0.3 = 2.42

Subtract From

Subtract 0.14 from 5.27.

Step 1: This problem uses the words *subtract* and *from*. This means you should begin with the second value, and subtract the first value. Write the problem in a column with the decimal points lined up.

$$
\begin{array}{r}
5.27 \\
-\ 0.14 \\
\end{array}
$$

Step 2: Subtract one place value at a time. Begin on the right. Subtract the hundredths.

$$
\begin{array}{r}
5.27 \\
-\ 0.14 \\
\hline
3 \\
\end{array}
$$

Step 3: Subtract the tenths.

$$
\begin{array}{r}
5.27 \\
-\ 0.14 \\
\hline
13 \\
\end{array}
$$

Step 4: Write the decimal point in the answer. Subtract the ones.

$$
\begin{array}{r}
5.27 \\
-\ 0.14 \\
\hline
5.13 \\
\end{array}
$$

TEST TIME: Multiple Choice

Vincent spent $16.22 on a DVD to watch with his 3 kids. When he took the same 3 kids to the movies, the total ticket price was $29.75. What is the difference in price between taking the kids to the movies and buying the DVD?

     a. $45.97

     b. $23.53

     c. $13.97

     d. $13.53

Write the numbers in a column. Line up the decimal points. Subtract.

$$\begin{array}{r} \$29.75 \\ - \ \$16.22 \\ \hline \$13.53 \end{array}$$

Solution: The correct answer is d.

19. Regrouping to Subtract

Regrouping in Subtraction

Subtract 6.3 − 2.6.

Step 1: Write the decimals in a column to line up the decimal points.

$$\begin{array}{r} 6.3 \\ -\ 2.6 \\ \hline \end{array}$$

Step 2: Subtract one place value at a time. Begin on the right. Look at the tenths place. You cannot subtract 6 from 3. Regroup 6 ones and 3 tenths as 5 ones and 13 tenths. Now you can subtract the tenths.

$$\begin{array}{r} 5\ \ 13 \\ \cancel{6}.\cancel{3} \\ -\ 2.6 \\ \hline 7 \end{array}$$

Step 3: Write the decimal point in the answer. Subtract the ones.

$$\begin{array}{r} 5\ \ 13 \\ \cancel{6}.\cancel{3} \\ -\ 2.6 \\ \hline 3.7 \end{array}$$

Definition

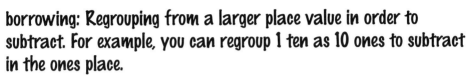

borrowing: Regrouping from a larger place value in order to subtract. For example, you can regroup 1 ten as 10 ones to subtract in the ones place.

TEST TIME: Multiple Choice

12.42 − 5.8 = _____

         (a.) 6.62

         b. 6.72

         c. 7.42

         d. 7.62

Write the numbers in a column. Line up the decimal points. Add zeros as placeholders.

$$
\begin{array}{r}
12.42 \\
-\ 5.80 \\
\hline
6.62
\end{array}
$$

Solution: The correct answer is a.

Subtracting with Zeros

Subtract 100 − 8.92.

Step 1: Write the decimals in a column to line up the decimal points. Add zeros to give each number the same number of decimal places.

$$\begin{array}{r} 100.00 \\ -\ \ \ \ 8.92 \\ \hline \end{array}$$

Step 2: You must regroup before you can subtract. There are no hundredths, tenths, ones, or tens to regroup. You can regroup 1 hundred as 9 tens, 9 ones, 9 tenths, and 10 hundredths.

$$\begin{array}{r} 9\ 9\ 9\ 10 \\ 100.00 \\ -\ \ \ \ 8.92 \\ \hline \end{array}$$

Step 3: Write the decimal point in the answer. Subtract in each place, from right to left. Remember to write the decimal point in the answer.

$$\begin{array}{r} 9\ 9\ 9\ 10 \\ 100.00 \\ -\ \ \ \ 8.92 \\ \hline 91.08 \end{array}$$

TEST TIME: Multiple Choice

A large cheese pizza costs $12.49.
A medium cheese pizza costs $9.99. An additional topping costs
$1.29 on a large and $0.98 on a medium. How much more does a
large one-topping pizza cost than a medium one-topping pizza?

(a.) **$2.81**
b. **$3.81**
c. **$10.97**
d. **$13.78**

**Before you can find the difference between the costs of the pizzas,
you must find the cost of each pizza. To solve a problem like this
quickly, you can use a calculator for each step.**

**A large one-topping pizza costs $12.49 + $1.29 = $13.78.
A medium one-topping pizza costs $9.99 + $0.98 = $10.97.
The difference is found by subtracting. $13.78 − $10.97 = $2.81.**

Solution: The correct answer is a.

Test-Taking Hint

When you use a calculator, you still need to understand
what to do with the numbers in the problem. A calculator
is only a tool, not a problem-solver.

20. Multiplying Decimals

Decimals and Whole Numbers

Decimals are multiplied in the same way as whole numbers.

Multiply 5 × 1.1.

Step 1: Ignore the decimal point and multiply as if both factors are whole numbers.

$$5 \times 1.1 = \underline{}$$
$$5 \times 11 = 55$$

Step 2: Count the number of decimal places after the decimal point in both factors.

5 has 0 decimal places. 1.1 has 1 decimal place. There is 1 decimal place in total.

Step 3: The total number of decimal places in the factors tells the number of decimal places in the product. Count one decimal place from the right. Place the decimal point in the answer.

$$5 \times 1.1 = 5.5$$

Definitions

factors: Numbers being multiplied.

product: The result of multiplication.

TEST TIME: Multiple Choice

Teri earns $7.50 per hour. If she worked 7 hours in one day, how much did she earn?

a. $48.50
b. $49.00
c. $50.50
(d.) $52.50

The word *per* in this problem tells you to use multiplication. You can quickly eliminate answers a and b by understanding that $7.50 is greater than $7.00, so $7.50 × 7 is greater than $49.00.

Multiply using either a calculator or a paper and pencil. $7.50 × 7 = $52.50.

Solution: The correct answer is d.

Decimals and Decimals

Multiply 4.7 × 0.02.

Step 1: Write the factors in a column. You do not need to line up the decimal points.

$$
\begin{array}{r}
4.7 \\
\times\ 0.02 \\
\hline
\end{array}
$$

Step 2: Ignore the decimal point and multiply as if both factors were whole numbers. Treat 0.02 as the whole number 2.

$$
\begin{array}{r}
4.7 \\
\times\ 0.02 \\
\hline
94
\end{array}
$$

Step 3: Count the number of decimal places in both factors.

4.7 has 1 decimal place. 0.02 has 2 decimal places. There are 3 decimal places in total.

Step 4: Count 3 decimal places from the right. There are only 2 decimal places in the product. Add a zero to the left to place the decimal point. Use a zero as a place holder in the ones place.

$$
\begin{array}{r}
4.7 \\
\times\ 0.02 \\
\hline
0.094
\end{array}
$$

TEST TIME: Show Your Work

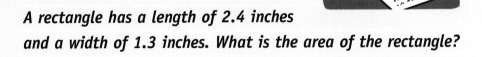

A rectangle has a length of 2.4 inches and a width of 1.3 inches. What is the area of the rectangle?

The area of a rectangle is found by multiplying the length by the width.

Solution:
$$
\begin{array}{r}
2.4 \text{ inches} \\
\times\ 1.3 \text{ inches} \\
\hline
72 \\
240 \\
\hline
3.12
\end{array}
$$

The area of the rectangle is 3.12 square inches.

Test-Taking Hint

Remember to include the units in your answers. Area problems always have square units.

21. Dividing Decimals

Dividing a Decimal

Gerard worked 9 days, for a total of 109.8 hours. How many hours did he average per day?

Step 1: Divide the total hours by the number of days. The long division symbol makes it easier to place the decimal point in decimal division. Write this problem using the long division symbol.

$$9 \overline{)109.8}$$

Step 2: Write the decimal point in the answer directly above the decimal point in the dividend.

$$9 \overline{)109.8}$$

Step 3: Divide as you would a whole number.

```
        12.2
   9 )109.8
     - 9
       19
     - 18
        18
      - 18
         0
```

Step 4: Write the answer in a complete sentence.

Gerard averaged 12.2 hours per day.

TEST TIME: Multiple Choice

1.8 ÷ 2 = ____

        a. 0.8

        b. 0.9

        c. 1.2

        d. 9

You can find this answer by knowing basic math facts and information about decimal multiplication. Ignore the decimal point. The basic fact is 18 ÷ 2 = 9, which is the same as 2 × 9 = 18. Knowing about decimal multiplication tells you there are the same number of decimal places in the product as there are in the factors. There is one decimal place.

Solution: The correct answer is b.

Dividing Whole Numbers and Decimals

Divide 2 ÷ 8.

Step 1: Write the problem using the long division symbol.

$$8\,)\overline{2}$$

Step 2: Write the number you are dividing as a decimal. Start with one zero. Place the decimal point in the answer.

$$8\,)\overline{2.0}^{\,.}$$

Step 3: Divide as you would a whole number. Add zeros and keep dividing until the remainder is zero.

$$
\begin{array}{r}
0.25 \\
8\,)\overline{2.00} \\
-16 \\
\hline
40 \\
-40 \\
\hline
0
\end{array}
$$

$2 ÷ 8 = 0.25$

Test-Taking Hint

Know your calculator. If you're using someone else's calculator, make sure you understand how to use it before you begin a test.

TEST TIME: Show Your Work

You have a choice of two packages of tank tops to buy. One has 3 tank tops for $12.96. The other has 2 tank tops for $8.98. Which is the better buy?

To find the better buy, you must find the cost of one tank top in each package. Divide each package cost by the number of tops in that package. You can use a calculator to find the cost per top, or you can divide on paper and check your work with a calculator.

Solution:　　$12.96 ÷ 3 = $4.32

　　　　　　　$8.98 ÷ 2 = $4.49

The package with 3 tank tops costs less per tank top, so it is the better buy.

22. Dividing by a Decimal

Decimals and Decimals

You can move the decimal point in a division problem as long as you move it the same way in both numbers.

Divide 0.6 ÷ 1.2.

Step 1: Write the problem using the long division symbol.

$$1.2\overline{)0.6}$$

Step 2: Before you begin, make the divisor a whole number by moving the decimal point one place to the right. Move the decimal point in the dividend the same number of places.

$$12.\overline{)06.0}$$

Step 3: Write the decimal point in the answer. Divide as you would a whole number.

$$
\begin{array}{r}
0.5 \\
12.\overline{)06.0} \\
-60 \\
\hline
0
\end{array}
$$

0.6 ÷ 1.2 = 0.5

TEST TIME: Multiple Choice

There are 1.6 kilometers in one mile. How many miles are there in 37.6 kilometers?

a. 21
b. 22.5
c. 23
d. 23.5

To find the number of miles in 37.6 kilometers, you must divide by the number of kilometers in one mile.
Divide using either a calculator or a paper and pencil.
37.6 ÷ 1.6 = 23.5

Solution: The correct answer is d.

Test-Taking Hint

Read word problems carefully. Key words such as "total," "per," "average," or "difference" can help you decide what operation should be performed.

Whole Numbers and Decimals

Divide 16 ÷ 0.5.

Step 1: Write the problem using the long division symbol.

$$0.5\overline{)16}$$

Step 2: Before you begin, make the divisor a whole number by moving the decimal point one place to the right. Move the decimal point in the dividend the same number of places. Remember, in a whole number like 16, the decimal point is at the end. Add zeros as needed to fill in the places on the right.

$$5\overline{)160}$$

Step 3: Now you have a whole number division problem. Divide.

$$
\begin{array}{r}
32 \\
5\overline{)160} \\
-15 \\
\hline
10 \\
-10 \\
\hline
0
\end{array}
$$

16 ÷ 0.5 = 32

TEST TIME: Show Your Work

A carpet has an area of 80 square feet.
The width of the carpet is 6.4 feet. What is the carpet's length?

The area of a carpet is found by multiplying length times width. When the area and one of the dimensions are given, you can find the missing dimension using division.

Solution: $80 \div 6.4$

$$6.4\overline{)80} = 64\overline{)800.0}$$

with the long division:

```
        12.5
 64 )800.0
    - 64
      160
    - 128
      320
    - 320
        0
```

The carpet is 12.5 feet long.

Test-Taking Hint

Check your answers whenever you can. In the problem above, you can check your answer using multiplication. $12.5 \times 6.4 = 80$. Correct!

23. Powers of Ten and Percents

TEST TIME: Explain Your Answer

Multiply 6.2 by 10, by 100, and by 1,000. Explain any patterns you see.

Solution: $6.2 \times 10 = 62$

$6.2 \times 100 = 620$

$6.2 \times 1,000 = 6,200$

In each equation, the digits stayed the same. The only difference was where the decimal point was. For each zero in the power of ten, the decimal point moved one place to the right.

Test-Taking Hint

Multiplication by a power of ten moves the decimal point to the right. Division by a power of ten moves the decimal point to the left.

Mental Multiplication

Multiply 1.32 by 10.

Step 1: You can multiply by a power of 10 using mental math. There is one zero in 10. Move the decimal point in the other factor one place right.

$$1.32 \times 10 = 13.2$$

Mental Division

Divide 82.6 by 100.

Step 1: You can divide by a power of 10 using mental math. There are two zeros in 100. Move the decimal point in the dividend two places left.

$$82.6 \div 100 = 0.826$$

Definition

percent: Out of 100. The percent sign means the same thing as a fractional denominator of 100. For example, 20% is the same as 20/100.

Percents

You can write decimals and fractions as percents.

Write 56/100 as a percent.

Step 1: The percent sign means the same thing as a denominator of 100. Write 56 and a percent sign.

56%

Write 0.72 as a percent.

Step 1: 0.72 is the same as 72/100. Any decimal can be written as a percent by moving the decimal point two places to the right.

72%

TEST TIME: Show Your Work

A bookstore has a super bargain rack with books that are 25% of the original price. What fraction of the original price are the books?

You can write a percent as a fraction by remembering the percent sign means the same thing as a denominator of 100.

Solution: $25\% = \dfrac{25}{100} = \dfrac{25 \div 25}{100 \div 25} = \dfrac{1}{4}$

The books are 1/4 of the original price.

Test-Taking Hint

You can go through a test and do the easy problems first. This can help you gain confidence, and keeps you from running out of time and missing easy points.

24. Rounding and Estimating

Estimating with Decimals

You can estimate with decimals by rounding the decimals to a whole number or to a set place value.

Estimate 12.4 × 8.8.

Step 1: Round each decimal to the nearest whole number.

12.4 rounds to 12
8.8 rounds to 9

Step 2: Multiply the rounded numbers.

12 × 9 = 108

Step 3: Remember when you write your answer that it is an estimate. Use words such as *about* or *around*.

12.4 × 8.8 is about 108.

Test-Taking Hint
Use estimation to check the results of exact answers.

TEST TIME: Multiple Choice

Round 16.89 to the tenths place.

> a. 20
> b. 17
> c. 16.9
> d. 16.8

Find the tenths place. The digit in the tenths place is 8. Look one place to the right, in the hundredths place. The digit in the hundredths place is 9. When the digit to the right is 5 or greater, you round up. Round 8 tenths up to 9 tenths.

Solution: The correct answer is c.

Definition

greatest place value: The first place from the left in a number that has a digit other than zero. For example, in the number 0.014 the first digit from the left that is not zero is the 1 in the hundredths place.

Greatest Place Value

Use rounding to the greatest place value to estimate 7.64 × 0.108.

Step 1: Round each number to its greatest place value.

The greatest place value in 7.64 is the ones place.

7.64 rounded to the ones place is 8.

The greatest place value in 0.108 is the tenths place.

0.108 rounded to the tenths place is 0.1.

Step 2: Multiply the rounded numbers.

$$8 \times 0.1 = 0.8$$
7.64 × 0.108 is about 0.8.

Step 3: Let's use a calculator to check the answer.

7.64 × 0.108 = 0.82512

TEST TIME: Show Your Work

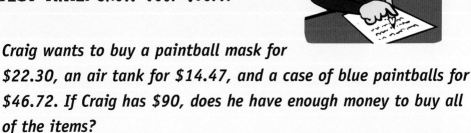

Craig wants to buy a paintball mask for $22.30, an air tank for $14.47, and a case of blue paintballs for $46.72. If Craig has $90, does he have enough money to buy all of the items?

To make sure you have enough of something, you can round all of the values up to the next whole dollar, then estimate. This is a high estimate, but you will have enough money to cover the cost.

Solution: $22.30 + $14.47 + $46.72
              $23 + $15 + $47 = $85

A high estimate of the cost is $85, and Craig has $90. Craig should have enough money to buy all of the items.

Test-Taking Hint

Make sure you are answering the question that is asked. Some problems require more than one step. In the problem above you must estimate the total cost, then compare the estimate to the amount Craig has to spend.

Further Reading

Books

Adler, David A. *Fractions, Decimals, and Percents*. New York: Holiday House, 2010.

McKellar, Danica. *Math Doesn't Suck: How to Survive Middle School Math Without Losing Your Mind or Breaking a Nail*. New York: Hudson Street Press, 2007.

Rozakis, Laurie. *Get Test Smart!: The Ultimate Guide to Middle School Standardized Tests*. New York: Scholastic Reference, 2007.

Internet Addresses

Banfill, J. *AAA Math.* 2009.
<http://www.aaastudy.com/dec.htm>

Coolmath.com, Inc. *Fraction Lessons.* 1997–2010.
<http://www.coolmath.com/prealgebra/01-fractions/index.html>

Testtakingtips.com. *Test Taking Tips.* 2003–2010.
<http://www.testtakingtips.com/test/math.htm>

Index

Index